Sugar Beet Crops

by Grace Hansen

Abdo Kids Jumbo is an Imprint of Abdo Kids
abdobooks.com

abdobooks.com

Published by Abdo Kids, a division of ABDO, P.O. Box 398166, Minneapolis, Minnesota 55439.
Copyright © 2024 by Abdo Consulting Group, Inc. International copyrights reserved in all countries.
No part of this book may be reproduced in any form without written permission from the publisher.
Abdo Kids Jumbo™ is a trademark and logo of Abdo Kids.

Printed in the United States of America, North Mankato, Minnesota.

052023

092023

THIS BOOK CONTAINS
RECYCLED MATERIALS

Photo Credits: Alamy, Getty Images, Granger Collection, Shutterstock,
United States Department of Agriculture

Production Contributors: Teddy Borth, Jennie Forsberg, Grace Hansen
Design Contributors: Victoria Bates, Candice Keimig

Library of Congress Control Number: 2022946808
Publisher's Cataloging-in-Publication Data

Names: Hansen, Grace, author.

Title: Sugar beet crops / by Grace Hansen

Description: Minneapolis, Minnesota : Abdo Kids, 2024 | Series: Agriculture in the USA! | Includes online
   resources and index.

Identifiers: ISBN 9781098266219 (lib. bdg.) | ISBN 9781098266912 (ebook) | ISBN 9781098267261
   (Read-to-me ebook)

Subjects: LCSH: Crops--Juvenile literature. | Agriculture--Juvenile literature. | Farming--Juvenile
   literature. | Field crops--Juvenile literature.

Classification: DDC 633.63--dc23

Table of Contents

Sweet Crop

Sugar beets are an important crop in the United States. They have special roots. The roots contain a lot of **sucrose**.

sugar
beet
farm
N
W E
S
OR
ID
MT
ND
MN
MI
WY
NE
CO
CA

The History of Sugar Beets

The beet plant has been around for centuries. Ancient cultures ate beet roots. In the 1700s, German scientist Andreas Marggraf learned that sugar could be taken from beet roots.

Andreas
Marggraf

In 1879, the first successful sugar beet factory opened in California. Sugar beet farms and factories quickly opened throughout the United States.

9

Growing Sugar Beets

Sugar is the main reason for growing sugar beets. The root is about 18% **sucrose**. It also contains 5% **pulp**. The pulp is used in animal feed.

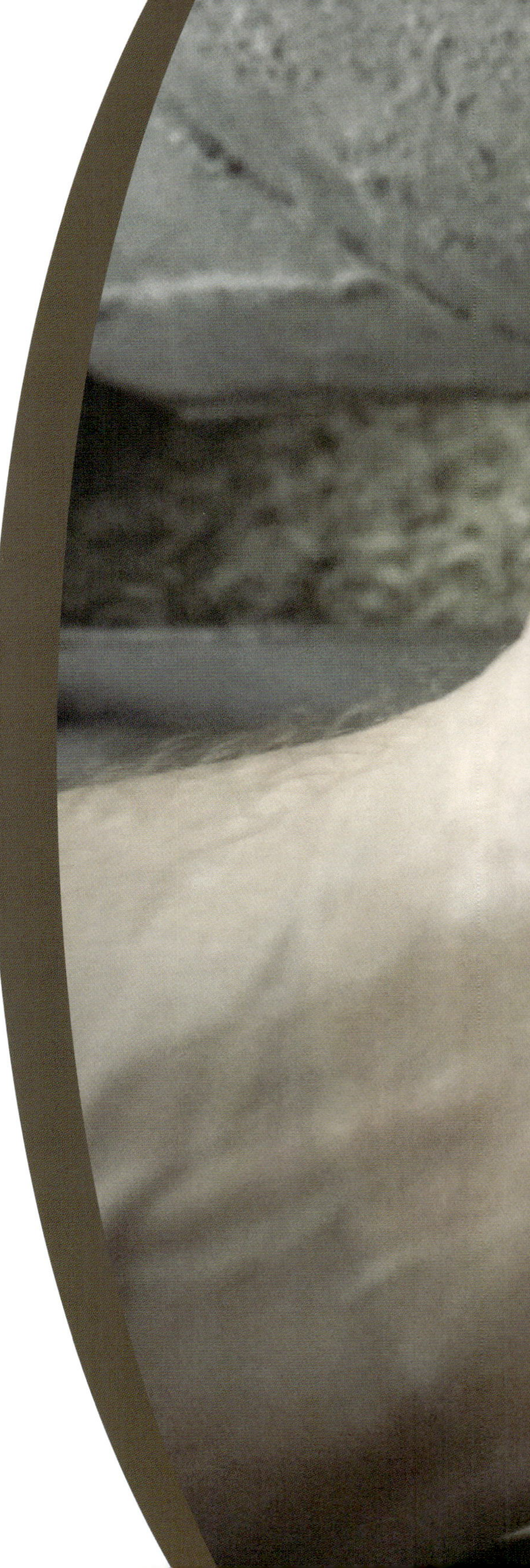

sugar beet pulp

Sugar beet farmers properly prepare their land and soil. The best soil for growing is rich in **humus**. This helps the soil hold moisture.

Farmers deeply plow their fields before planting seeds. This allows sugar beet roots to grow down into the loose soil.

In cooler regions of the United States, sugar beets are planted in spring. In areas that stay warmer year round, sugar beets are planted in the fall.

Sugar beets take 170 to 200 days to grow. A fully-grown sugar beet is about 1 foot (.3 m) long. It can weigh 2 to 5 pounds (.9-2.2 kg).

MAXTRON
620

The sugar beets are **harvested** and taken to nearby factories. They are washed, sliced, and **processed** into sugar. The sugar is stored in silos until it is ready to package.

Sugar Beet Growth Stages

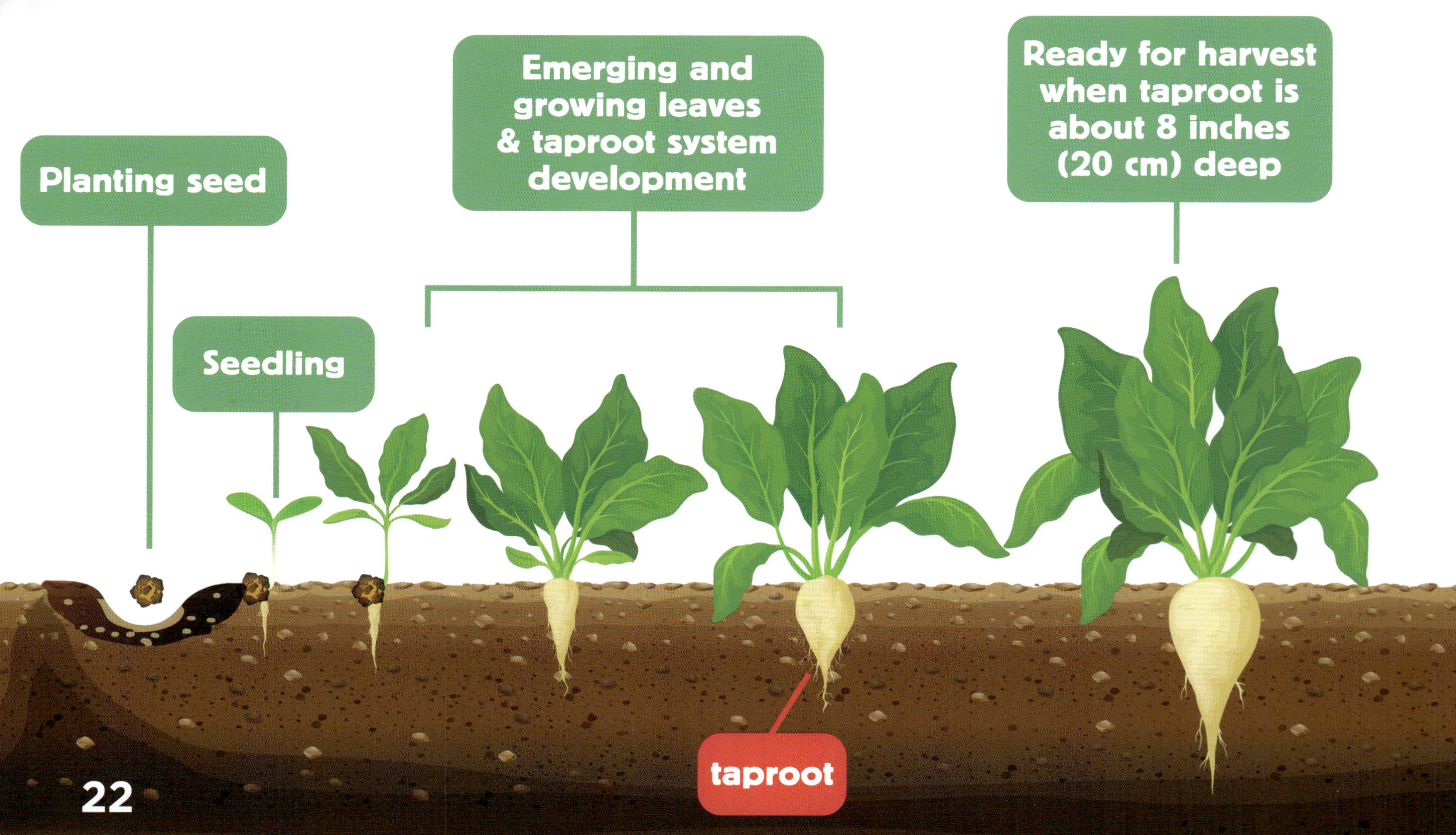

Glossary

harvest – the gathering of ripe crops, the crops or the amount of crops gathered, or the season in which they are gathered.

humus – a material made up of partly decayed leaves and plants. Humus adds nutrients to soil and helps it hold water.

processed – treated or prepared by a particular series of actions.

pulp – a soft mass of vegetable matter from which most of the water has been taken out.

sucrose – a type of sugar obtained from sugar beets and sugar cane.

Index

Abdo Kids
ONLINE
FREE! ONLINE MULTIMEDIA RESOURCES

Visit **abdokids.com** to access crafts, games, videos, and more!

Use Abdo Kids code **ASK6219** or scan this QR code!